What Happened to the Dinosaurs?

Written and
il
Jo

Contents

Collins

What were the dinosaurs?

Most people have heard about dinosaurs. They know that millions of years ago huge creatures roamed the Earth, bigger than any land animal found today. There were small dinosaurs too – but it's dinosaurs like the giant **Tyrannosaurus Rex** that have captured people's imagination.

But where are the dinosaurs today? About 65 million years ago they simply seemed to disappear. Have you ever wondered *why* these gigantic creatures died out? No one knows for sure, but there are clues. This book looks at these clues to try to work out what happened.

Dinosaurs only lived on land and not in the sea, and their name, "dino-saur", means "terrible lizard". They were a kind of **reptile**, but they weren't like the lizards and snakes that you see today.

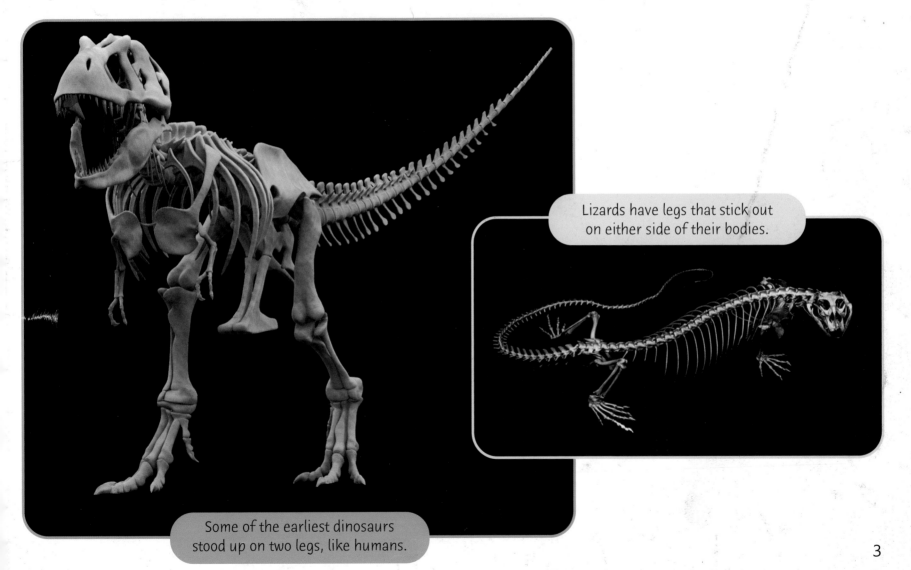

Lizards have legs that stick out on either side of their bodies.

Some of the earliest dinosaurs stood up on two legs, like humans.

Dinosaurs lived on Earth for over 180 million years.

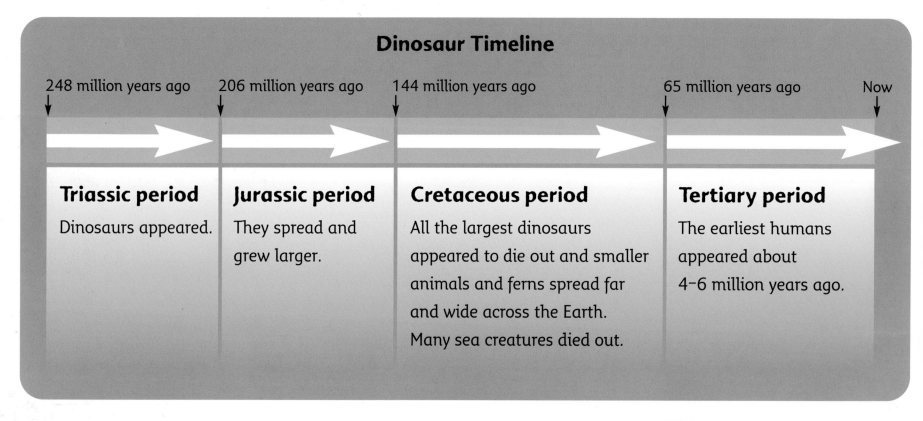

Dinosaur Timeline

248 million years ago	206 million years ago	144 million years ago	65 million years ago	Now
Triassic period Dinosaurs appeared.	**Jurassic period** They spread and grew larger.	**Cretaceous period** All the largest dinosaurs appeared to die out and smaller animals and ferns spread far and wide across the Earth. Many sea creatures died out.	**Tertiary period** The earliest humans appeared about 4–6 million years ago.	

How do we know they existed?

We know that dinosaurs existed because scientists have found dinosaur fossils in rocks around the world. Over time, rocks form layers and each layer tells a story. If scientists can work out how old the rock is, then they can tell when the dinosaur was alive. They can also tell which plants were around at the same time.

What is a fossil?

Over millions of years, the hard parts of an animal – its bones and teeth – can turn to stone. Sometimes, even the damp mud where it walked can turn to stone and scientists have found fossils of dinosaur footprints.

1 A fossil forms when an animal dies and is quickly buried with a layer of sand or mud.

2 Water containing **minerals** trickles over the bones.

3 Over time, the bones become stone.

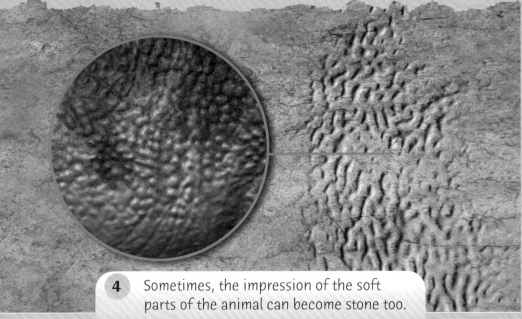

4 Sometimes, the impression of the soft parts of the animal can become stone too.

5 Plants or even footsteps can also become fossilised.

The fossil, together with the layer of rock where the fossil was found, gives us the fossil record and that gives us vital clues about what happened in the past. However, not many animals become fossils. Most die and are eaten or simply turn to dust. This means that we can only find out about a few animals. There must be many kinds of dinosaur that have disappeared forever, which we'll never know about.

7

The world at the time of the dinosaurs

To find out why these creatures died out, scientists have been discovering what the world was like when the dinosaurs were around. It wasn't like it is today.

The **climate** was warmer and the North and South Poles weren't frozen. There were many trees and plants, although they were different from the ones that grow today, and the plant-eating creatures grew to an enormous size. The meat-eating animals also grew big because there was plenty for them to eat too.

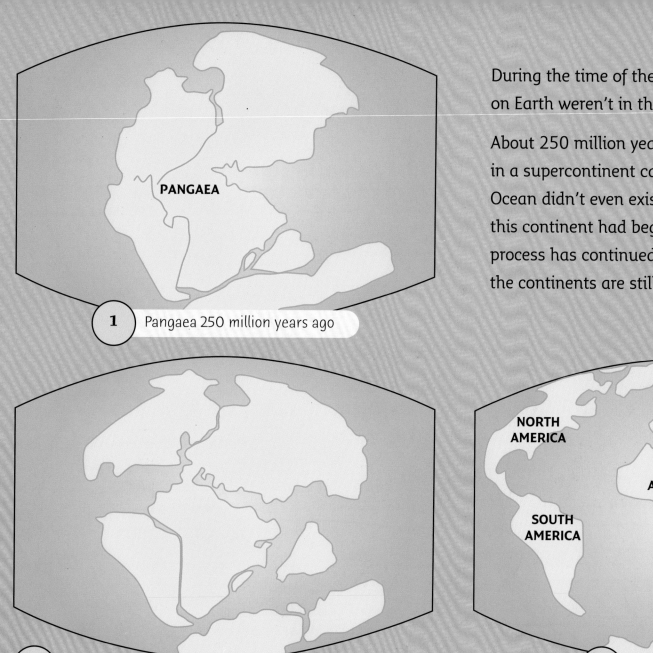

During the time of the dinosaurs, the **continents** on Earth weren't in the same place as they are today.

About 250 million years ago they were stuck together in a supercontinent called Pangaea. The Atlantic Ocean didn't even exist. By the Jurassic period, this continent had begun to break up and this process has continued until the present day. In fact, the continents are still moving, but very, very slowly.

PANGAEA

1 Pangaea 250 million years ago

2 The continents breaking up during the Jurassic period

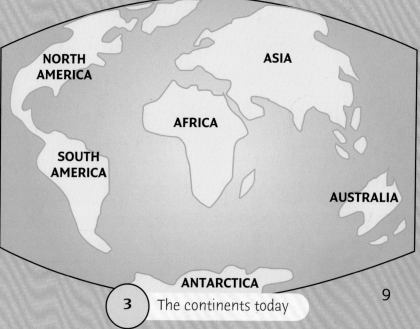

NORTH AMERICA

ASIA

AFRICA

SOUTH AMERICA

AUSTRALIA

ANTARCTICA

3 The continents today

9

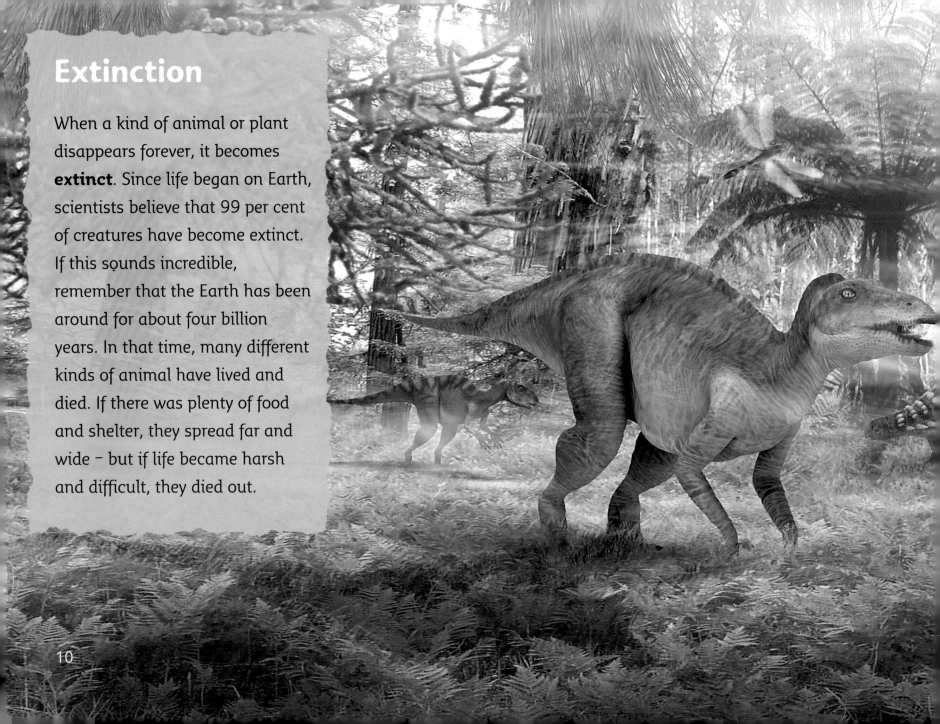

Extinction

When a kind of animal or plant disappears forever, it becomes **extinct**. Since life began on Earth, scientists believe that 99 per cent of creatures have become extinct. If this sounds incredible, remember that the Earth has been around for about four billion years. In that time, many different kinds of animal have lived and died. If there was plenty of food and shelter, they spread far and wide – but if life became harsh and difficult, they died out.

Animals can become extinct in two ways. They can die out slowly over many millions of years, or much more quickly, over hundreds of years.

Some scientists think that the dinosaurs became extinct slowly. Others think they went out with a bang.

Changing climate

Scientists have a reason for thinking that the dinosaurs became extinct slowly.

They know that the Earth's continents were splitting up and moving at this time. They also know that there were big changes in the climate on Earth towards the end of the age of the dinosaurs. The weather became colder and the warm, shallow seas began to dry up. These changes probably meant that dinosaurs had to travel long distances to find food.

Some plants died out and new ones developed. If a dinosaur only ate a kind of plant that died out, the dinosaur would have died out too.

12

Volcanoes

Other scientists have reasons for thinking that the dinosaurs became extinct more quickly. They know that at this time there were many active volcanoes because the signs of these volcanoes are still here today. They believe that a place called the Deccan Traps in India had huge volcanic eruptions at this time.

When volcanoes erupt, they send many millions of tonnes of ash and rock into the air. This can make the weather cooler because sunlight can't reach the Earth.

Volcanoes also pour out poisonous gas, steam and rocks that destroy life for hundreds of kilometres around.

Poisonous gas from volcanoes can destroy the oxygen in the air. All animals need oxygen to breathe. Scientists have found air bubbles trapped in amber from this time and have measured the oxygen in these bubbles. They discovered that at the time the dinosaurs died out, there was less oxygen in the air. If the dinosaurs couldn't breathe properly, they would certainly have died.

Amber is fossilised **resin** from trees.

Other scientists point out that when some dinosaurs died, they seemed to be sick. Did the dinosaurs get ill because of the poisonous gas? Or were they already weak and ill, because they couldn't find enough food?

Asteroids

Some scientists have another reason for thinking that the big dinosaurs may have died out quite quickly. They believe that something happened, suddenly and in one place, that made life impossible for them.

They believe that an **asteroid** from outer space hit the Earth. Even a small asteroid a few kilometres wide would have caused enormous damage. It would have sent millions of tonnes of boiling rock and gas into the air, like a vast volcanic eruption. It would have caused several gigantic **tsunamis** as the hot rocks fell back into the sea. Waves a hundred metres high would have surged over the land.

The asteroid would have killed everything close by, and many living things around the world – but some animals and plants would have survived if they were a long way from where the asteroid struck.

What clues are there?

In Mexico, near the sea, there's a huge **crater** about 180 kilometres across, which was formed about 65 million years ago – at the time when the dinosaurs were dying out. It could have been made by an asteroid about 17 kilometres across striking the Earth. There are also signs of huge waves and floods in that area at that time. Some scientists also think that other asteroids may have struck in other parts of the Earth.

Some people think that when the asteroids struck, the Earth was in darkness for months as the air was full of ash and dust. It got colder and the amount of oxygen in the air fell. Plants died, and plant-eating dinosaurs died because they couldn't find enough food. Then meat-eating dinosaurs also died.

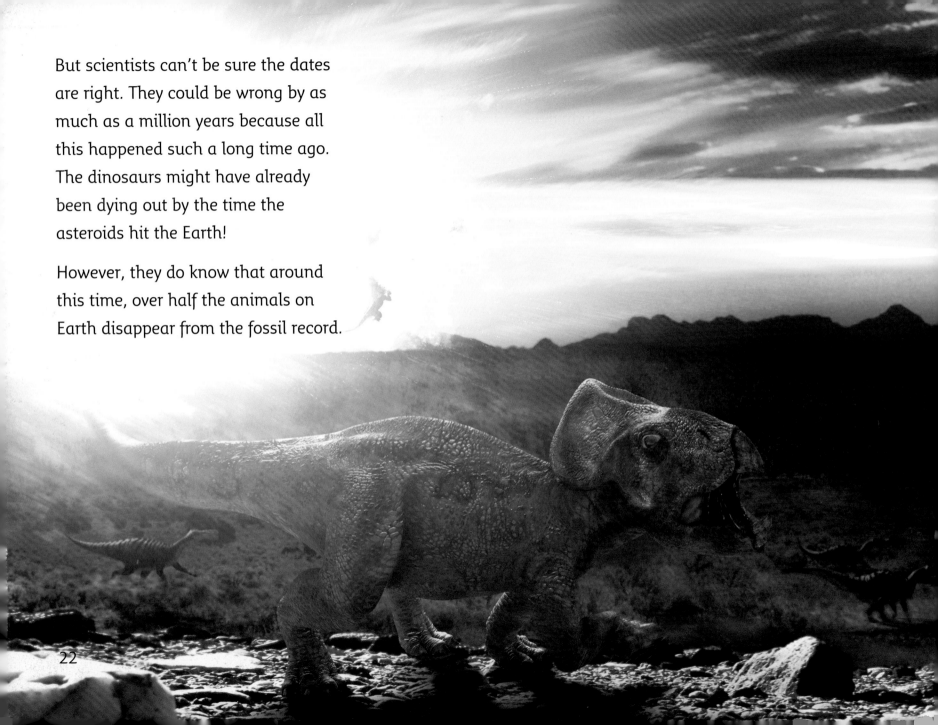

But scientists can't be sure the dates are right. They could be wrong by as much as a million years because all this happened such a long time ago. The dinosaurs might have already been dying out by the time the asteroids hit the Earth!

However, they do know that around this time, over half the animals on Earth disappear from the fossil record.

It wasn't only dinosaurs that disappeared. Animals that flew, like the **pterosaurs**, died and so did animals that lived in the seas, such as the **plesiosaurs**. Most large animals died, including **mammals** and reptiles.

It was the small creatures that survived, developed and in time spread over the Earth.

Dinosaur birds

Recently, scientists have been looking again at the fossil record. They now think that some small dinosaurs *didn't* become extinct. They developed into birds! Scientists think this because:

- The skeletons of birds and dinosaurs are very similar. For example, the meat-eating **velociraptor** has bones similar to a large bird.

- Both birds and dinosaurs lay eggs.

- Some dinosaur fossils have been found with feathers.

Next time you see an ostrich or an emu, think how they may be related to dinosaurs.

More to discover

The dinosaurs lived successfully on Earth for many millions of years. It seems likely that they died out for several different reasons. The climate was changing and there were very many active volcanoes. Perhaps asteroids did strike the Earth from outer space, but by that time many dinosaurs had already become extinct. Perhaps the asteroids simply speeded things up.

The answer lies buried under the ground in the ancient rocks of the fossil record. We'll need to find a lot more fossils before we discover the truth about the disappearing dinosaurs.

Glossary

asteroid   a large piece of rock or metal, which moves around the sun

climate   the long-term weather conditions of an area

continents   the large areas of land on the Earth

crater   the bowl-shaped opening at the top or side of a volcano

extinct   having died out

mammals   animals with warm blood, which have hair and give birth to live young

minerals   natural, non-living substances, like gold or copper

plesiosaurs   marine reptiles, with long necks, short, pointed tails and limbs like flippers

pterosaurs   flying reptiles that lived during the time of the dinosaurs

reptile   a cold-blooded animal with a backbone and an outer covering of horny scales and plates

resin   a liquid produced by plants, which hardens in the air

tsunamis   giant sea waves caused by an earthquake under the sea or a volcanic eruption

Tyrannosaurus Rex   a fierce, meat-eating dinosaur with long, sharp teeth and powerful jaws

velociraptor   a fast-running, meat-eating dinosaur with sharp teeth and two legs

Index

To find out the names of all the dinosaurs in this book, visit www.collinsbigcat.com and follow the links.

What happened to the dinosaurs?

They could have died out because the climate changed and they could no longer find food.

They could have been poisoned when many volcanoes erupted.